W. D. Griffith

Hooray for Retirement!

What you have always wanted to know about life and living.

Illustrated by Roland Rodegast

Published by
The C. R. Gibson Company
Norwalk, Connecticut

Foreword

This book is based on numerous
one-liners, quotes, and other data concerning
life which have appeared and
reappeared in various printed media during
the past fifteen years or so.

Whether bringing them together here,
in narrative form, will have any influence
on the thinking of those millions
who can not escape eventual retirement,
can only be left to the imagination.

To each originator, columnist, and
editor, whoever and wherever you are,
thanks for the morsels of wit, wisdom,
and just plain facts, which have helped
so much in the edification
of the American public.

W. D. GRIFFITH

Contents

Chapter 1.

Preamble

People who don't know where they are going usually wind up somewhere else, so ask yourself this question: "Where am *I* headed as I whiz through life at the rate of 3,600 seconds an hour? Am I like a pin, pointed in one direction, and headed in another?" Not at all! You're headed in one direction only — toward *retirement!* This is true even of the person who seems so well rounded he isn't pointed in any direction.

And you have plenty of company, for at the present average rate of 4,900 people reaching age sixty-five any day this year, you would have 4,899 companions (give or take a few). By 1980, this average daily rate will be more than 5,000; for the year 2000, your guestimate is as good as your neighbor's.

Of course, there are some who retire earlier — much earlier — in fact, soon after they are born. They handle life as they do bad weather — just whiling away the time waiting for it to stop. Others, failing to realize the only difference between a rut and a grave is its depth, seem to manage to keep their heads above water because wood floats. And there are still others who keep afloat by taking advantage of a raft of friends.

There are even many people, born with silver spoons in their mouths, who haven't stirred since. Such persons make the authorities look good who claim man can exist without air for seven minutes, without water for seven days, without food for seven weeks, and without brains for seventy years. For them, age sixty-five means nothing more than another year they have struggled through, and the future is only more of the same.

Others never seem to retire. They know the years don't come to be counted; they come to count for something. They keep their yesterdays filed away, their present in order, and their future subject to instant revision. Such people can roll with the punches. They know that if a man doesn't get happier as he gets older, he hasn't learned what he should have along the way. They keep in mind that although one can't change one's ancestors, one *can* do something about his descendants.

Broadly speaking, you'll find life is split into three stages: youth, middle age, and the time when people say, "My, but you're looking well!" Youth is the time for looking ahead and thinking you'll live forever; retirement years are for looking back; middle age is the inbetween period when you merely look startled and wonder how you've lasted as long as you have.

Through each of these stages you'll encounter some people who make things happen, some who watch things happen, and others who don't know that anything has happened! What you get

5

out of life will depend largely on how you are classified. Of course, like others, you'll have your personal problems and frustrations. But if you'll just remember that man, like a bridge, was designed to carry the load of the moment, not the combined weight of a year at once, you should pull through with a plus score.

Two things you'll have plenty of in life are good advice and bad example. But if you listen to too much advice, you'll wind up making other people's mistakes; besides, if you can tell the difference between good advice and bad advice, you don't need advice in the first place. As for bad examples, you'll probably discover that much of mankind are mere imitators of very poor originals. So don't pay much attention to either.

With no blueprint of life to follow, most of us feel alone in a crowd; and directions won't help, for they are what we read too late to see what we did wrong. To be honest, most of us would rather risk catastrophe than read directions. But we definitely need some kind of aid, something for comparison as we move along, if we're to agree with George Washington who said, "Retirement is as necessary to me as it is welcome."

So possibly this candid and rather off-beat look at that road we all travel, sprinkled with comments and experiences of others, will help. Above all, never let the future scare you. It's just as shaky as you are. And fortunately, it comes only a day at a time.

Chapter 2.

The first nine years.

It is estimated that America's population increases by one person every ten and a half seconds. Although we haven't yet controlled the population explosion, we have it timed. Thus, when the bundle from heaven arrives, he immediately is endowed with life, liberty, and a substantial share of the national debt.

The day a person is born, everybody in the world will be older than he is. When he is twenty-six years old, there will be just as many people younger than he is as there are older. That will be the half-way point. When he is forty years old, 80 per cent of them will be younger.

A child comes into the world with a brain which, if properly developed, can become a honey of a computer. It has several

billion circuits; and when he grows up, it can operate for hours on the energy contained in a single peanut. The brain is completely mobile, occupies less than a cubic foot of space, and is produced by unskilled labor. What a bargain!

As you review the past, you appreciate how true it is that childhood chews hours and swallows minutes. You also realize how inconsistent parents are when they spend the first part of a child's life urging him to walk and talk, and the rest of his childhood getting him to sit down and keep quiet. And you sympathize with the parent who said, "I sure wish someone would invent a vitamin for children that includes B-1, B-2 and B-Quiet."

Then the kid goes to kindergarten and, being confused as to his status, asks a little girl, "Are you the opposite sex, or am I?" After kindergarten he begins his regular school years and has to travel farther than his ancestors went on vacation. As you look back, you see how really tough kids have it today. Where you used to walk to school, and kept warm by running part of the way, now they stand and shiver waiting for the bus.

Teachers have their problems, too. One in the early grades continually reminds herself, "Think small." In the middle grades, another teacher laments, "Not only is he the worst behaved child in my class, but he has a perfect attendance record." Still another reports about a student: "Dull, but steady — would make a good parent." In the later grades a father, after looking over a report card, compliments his son, "One thing's in your favor — with these grades you couldn't possibly be cheating."

Finally, you can tell a child is growing up when he stops asking where he came from and starts refusing to tell where he is going. It is also about this time, as he passes from childhood and becomes a teenager, that you find heredity is what makes the mother and father wonder a little about each other.

Chapter 3.

The teenage years.

These are the years that are often called the rehearsal time on the stage of life. It is the period when the key to success is the one that fits the ignition; the early bird gets a parking place close to the school; and walking distance is between the telephone and garage. And it's the time when a girl confides to her girl friend regarding her date: "He likes to park, but doesn't know why."

Teenage years are problem years for parents. The youngsters need guidance, but are developing personalities of their own. As one parent put it, "When our son was a baby, he slept days and was awake at nights; and now that he's a teenager, he's working hard for the same rights."

Some parents feel an allowance is what they pay their children for living with them; other parents feel parents were invented to make children happy by giving them something to ignore. Perhaps the relationship of host and guest is the happiest solution. And, if you find your own teenager is also a parent-ager, possibly the best way to recapture your youth is to cut off his allowance.

A father often admits his son is at the awkward age — too old for spanking and too young for analysis. He also wonders what kind of an "in" crowd the boy travels with — in doubt, in debt, or in trouble.

During this period, the parent who wants his children to get a high school education may find he has to pull a few wires — the television wire, the hi-fi wire, and the radio wire. He knows that many a child who watches television for hours will go down in history — not to mention arithmetic, English and geography. But in school you'll find chivalry is not dead. If a teenage girl drops one of her books, almost any boy in the class will kick it back to her.

Talking to his son about the need for a good education, a father explains, "Either you have to go to college, or start a business of your own so that you can hire the people who did." And an all-wise son might reply, "Yes, I know. I've got to learn a skill so I'll know what kind of work I'm out of." Years later he finds out that an education is something you get when your father sends you to college, but isn't complete until you send your own son there.

With her teenage daughter, a mother has her problems. First she gets irritated, and cautions, "You behave yourself, or I'll let down all your hems." But it isn't long until she is exclaiming, "Oh, they grow up so fast. My daughter is already wearing her first long pants."

When the daughter goes to college, the mother tells a friend: "I couldn't help thinking as we paid the tuition deposit that we're losing a daughter, but gaining a closet." And during these four years the parents find it is true that two can live as cheaply as one, provided the one is a daughter in college.

As a whole, though, teenagers haven't changed much. They still grow up, leave home, and get married. The big difference is that today they don't always do it in that order. However, there's nothing wrong with the younger generation that becoming tax-payers won't cure.

Chapter 4

The twenties.

You recall the twenties. Wonderful years full of enthusiasm and confused thinking. Still too young to know that the difference between genius and stupidity is simply that genius has its limits.

It's the time when a young man hesitates to take out a straight life insurance policy because he still wants to fool around some on weekends. His spirit is dampened temporarily when he finds the only job where he can start at the top is digging a hole.

For the young woman, these are the years when the thought of marriage is uppermost. As an animal lover, she knows that after her twenties are history and she's still single, she may be more on the lookout for a silver fox or a short balding wolf — and neither

has a romantic ring. What she really wants is to be swept off her feet by someone she can dominate.

She also knows she has to play smart to get a job, dumb to get a husband, that her chief asset is a man's imagination, and a bikini is a suit used more for hunting than for swimming. And after attracting the man she wants, she hums to herself, "I'll bristle with rollers and pin curls; I'll slither with slippery creams; and nightly turn into a nightmare, to remain the girl of your dreams." To her girl friend she admits, "He was dressed just the way I like to see a man — no wedding ring."

Some marriages happen rather quickly, like that of the young couple who had known each other only a few days. When he asked, "Do you think you could learn to love me?", she replied timidly, "I think so. I learned shorthand in three weeks." Others are the result of something like computer programming, where the young man is hooked by a calculating mother.

But most marriages take longer to come about because the young man feels he wants to be his own boss. He has thoughts of remaining a bachelor and, during this period, about the only golden opportunities he recognizes are blondes. Not so much because men prefer blondes, but because they can be seen better and quicker.

This situation seldom endures, however. Although he may have sworn to remain a bachelor, *she'd* sworn to be a bride, and of course you've guessed the answer — she had nature on her side. All she needed was a little time, for even the wisest men make fools of themselves over women, and even the most foolish women are wise about men. Indeed, almost any woman knows a man is but a worm. He comes along, wriggles a bit, and then some chicken gets him.

Later, the new husband confides to a friend, "For months on

end we table hopped. Man, did we ever do the town! We lived it up until I dropped — and then she tied me down." Too late he finds that in marriage, as in boxing, the preliminaries are often more entertaining than the main event.

After a few months as a husband, he admits, "Ever since I said, 'I do,' there are so many things I don't." But privately he had good reasons for becoming a twosome. He found car insurance is higher for single men; evidently insurance companies feel getting married isn't such a reckless step as he had imagined. He also decided it would be better to give up half his groceries in order to get the other half cooked.

Furthermore, he found out that, as a typical bachelor, he was spending about 408 hours a year on housework, which he was most willing to turn over to his bride. So they became engaged, and after selecting an engagement ring, the girl exclaimed, "Isn't it romantic — our first time payment!"

After marriage, there are some four-letter words which usually shock a bride — like cook, mend, wash, and iron. One newlywed was heard to exclaim to another, "Marriage is really a grind. You wash dishes, change bedding — then two weeks later you have to do it all over again." To make their marriage work, both find it is like running a farm — you have to start all over again each morning. It is also something like the army — everybody complains, but you'd be surprised how many re-enlist.

Chapter 5

The thirties.

Then come the critical thirties. These are the peak years and physically, from here on, it is all down hill. If our retiree-to-be is a family man, he finds he is replacing the currency in his billfold with snapshots. Labor saving devices and other items are purchased until he finally learns there is a monthly installment due every day. He confides in a friend, "No, I don't go skiing any more. I'm going down hill fast enough as it is."

Only a husband who is a wizard can keep up with the neighbors and the installments, too. But he isn't licked, for of all the appointments, conveniences, and gadgets around the house, the most useful is still the good old checkbook. (And many wives figure it takes four check-books to fill one book of trading stamps.) So he

does some figuring and finds if he misses two payments on the washer-drier, and one on the refrigerator, he'll have enough for a down payment on a TV set.

Yes sir! Give a man credit for anything — and he'll buy it! No wonder the American male is often depressed by the awful fear of not belonging. His car doesn't belong to him; his house doesn't belong to him; his furniture doesn't belong to him, and on and on. And, oddly enough, research shows that tall men are as short at the end of the month as anyone else.

When he reaches thirty-five, the average man has a life expectancy of 17,000,000 minutes. Yet he might gamble all that time to save a single minute in traffic. Some odds — 1 to 17,000,000. So keep that statistic in mind the next time *you* feel frustrated in traffic — it might calm you down and save you from a bad situation. One bad gamble could eliminate further aging completely.

By his late thirties, our retiree-to-be should have accepted the fact that the only things perfect mates come in are shoes and gloves, unless he knows a couple where the wife is a hypochondriac and the husband is a pill. He finds he gets along better if he brings home a little applesauce with the bacon; the wife has learned keeping her husband in hot water doesn't make him tender. And both of them gradually learn that the bonds of matrimony are like any other bonds — they take a while to mature.

Chapter 6.

The forties.

The forties are considered the early years of middle age. Although it may be true that life begins at forty, so does arthritis, lumbago, and the habit of telling a story three times to the same group. It is also the time when everything else starts to wear out, fall out, or spread out. You suddenly realize a man's hair is limited to three styles — parted, unparted, and departed. The big trouble with life is that you are half way through it before realizing it's one of those do-it-yourself deals.

The forties are called middle age because the middle is where it usually shows most. It is the time when your memory is shorter, your experience longer, your stamina lower, and your forehead higher. The children leave you one by one, only to return two by

two. You still have the old spark, but it takes more puffing. Whether your mind and body reach middle age at the same time may depend on how active you are, for scientists say that an inactive man's body reaches middle age physiologically not at forty-five, but at about twenty-six.

Looking toward the future and knowing your health is most important if you still have half of your life ahead of you, you decide to go to your doctor for a checkup. When one fellow did this, the conversation went something like this:

"Do you think I'll live until I'm ninety, doctor?"

"How old are you now?"

"Forty."

"Do you drink, gamble, smoke, or have any vices of any kind?"

"No I don't drink, I never gamble, I loathe smoking. In fact, I haven't any vices."

"Well, then, why do you want to live another fifty years?"

Vices, dreams — there must be something in the future to make it seem worthwhile. Otherwise, you may develop a most serious physical defect — no guts.

The forties bring the middle years. These middle years make up that quiet, peaceful, serene period between completing the children's education and starting to help with the first grandchildren. These middle years generally last from three to five months.

As a whole, middle age is that difficult period between juvenile delinquency and senior citizenship when you have to take care of yourself — and intend to begin any day now. The big shock is that you keep growing older, even after you are old enough. You find the go-go girl you married in her twenties has become the chug-chug girl of her forties. As the years pass, you think of resigning from the jet set to join the set set.

During this period, we accept (ever so grudgingly) the responsibility that we are here in the world to help others, but continue to wonder what the others are here for. You wouldn't mind the meek inheriting the earth, if you could be sure they would stay meek after they got it. But, supposing they didn't have the nerve to refuse and did take over, who would drive the trucks and buses? Ask the young and the old, for they have all the answers — you're only stuck with the questions.

Even so, middle-agers are said to be like Mexican burros. They carry an incredible load, and receive a good many kicks to boot. They are expected to make vital decisions that guide the biggest business enterprises, the churches, the schools, and other bulwarks of society. Yet it is constantly dinned into their ears that a man or woman over forty can't get a job.

This over-forty attitude should never have developed, and employers would do well to spearhead a change. For even at fifty-five, U.S. Labor Department statistics show that the average person stays on a new job longer than the twenty-five year old, absenteeism is considerably lower in the older age group, and productivity is at least equal in each wage bracket. So, if you're over forty and capable, go ahead and do some dinning of your own.

Chapter 7.

From fifty on.

By the time the average man reaches fifty, he has slept 6,000 days, worked 7,500 days, was sick 500 days, and amused himself 4,000 days. That leaves only about 250 days spent on education, religion, and other pursuits. However, if they were spent wisely, they will pay worthwhile dividends during the years ahead.

Most of us keep an eye on the temptations we pray not to be led into. But after passing fifty, you needn't worry so much about avoiding them — that's when they start avoiding you. Besides, the Devil is easy to identify. He appears when you are terribly tired, and makes reasonable requests you know you shouldn't grant.

After fifty, your thoughts turn more often to the friendships you

enjoy — even including the friend who is always around when he needs you. It also comforts you that, as a group, your friends include those who know all about you, but remain your friends just the same. You can easily separate the people you know (and have known) into two groups — those who cause happiness wherever they go, the others whenever they go. And speaking of friendships, it is all right to use them as drawing accounts if you wish, as long as you don't forget the deposits.

At fifty you look back and recall that in your twenties you wanted to save the world; now you're satisfied if you can just save part of your salary. All through the years, you've found that the hardest thing about making money last — is making it first. And there have been times you've discovered that inflation is when, after you get the money to buy something, it isn't enough. However, although money can't buy love, health, happiness, or what it did last year, you still find it keeps creditors in a better frame of mind.

For many reasons, these are the years when a marriage can be severely tested. After having lived together for so many years, it is only natural for each spouse to get on the other's nerves now and then. This happens mostly because the average man will lose his temper about six times a week, while the average woman loses hers only three times — probably because wives don't get mad, they get even. But temper is a funny thing — you can't get rid of it by losing it.

In marriage, too, little things can be ballooned out of proportion when they are remembered and multiplied. For example, a couple starts out for the evening, and the wife admonishes, "Now if it's a dull party, just leave it that way." Or he says, "You'd make a good umpire — you never think I'm safe when I'm out." When she comes home laden with packages and says, "I'll tell you what

21

happened to our nest egg. This old hen got tired of sitting on it," he counters with, "I'll swear you've gone from hard-to-get to hard-to-handle to hard-to-take." Then one evening she says, "Here's your dinner, darling, prepared the way you'd better like it."

These are nothing more than momentary flareups, but their continuity hits a nerve and, if the husband feels he is overly abused, he may think a separation is the answer. However, when he finds money for a divorce doesn't come under home-improvement loans, and a friend tells him alimony is a splitting headache, he has second thoughts.

Rarely do such situations reach a climax, but when one does, possibly the best solution is a second honeymoon — with him going in July and her in August. The next best thing would be for the wife to buy a button-up-the back dress, for nothing else can do so much to bring a husband and wife together. And she might just do it, for although a woman may not be as logical as a man, she is often a step ahead of him in her thinking.

At any rate, the fifties gradually slide into the sixties, and at last the so-called golden years arrive. When they do, that period of life in which many of us have spent the first six days of the week sowing wild oats, then going to church on Sunday to pray for a crop failure, is behind us.

A new way of life lies ahead and if it were true that the brain is like a sponge, you might wish you could squeeze yours once in a while to get rid of the stuff you don't need any more. And you might be able to get rid of plenty, for the human brain, which weighs about three pounds, is said to be capable of holding enough information to fill six million books.

Chapter 8

How to tell you're aging.

The first proof that you're aging is when you think other people aren't having the fun you had. Another sure sign is when you feel like the day after the night before — and you haven't been anywhere.

You can also tell you're getting older when your wife turns off the alarm clock while you're still sleepy, and says, "Think of it this way — you're a day closer to Social Security and Medicare." She probably doesn't know the average man needs forty-five minutes more sleep than the average woman, and that his metabolism, on waking, gets off to a much slower start. But just as going to bed can cure half of one's ills, getting up can remedy the other half. So, up and at 'em. If you can be pleasant until ten o'clock in the morning,

the rest of the day will take care of itself.

The years are also piling up *if:*

— everybody calls you Dad except your own children;

— the girls where you work start confiding in you;

— keeping a secret gives you more satisfaction than passing it along;

— you have the shape for the job, but the kids no longer believe in Santa Claus;

— you can remember when "extras" were special newspaper editions, instead of a thousand or so dollars added to the price of a new car.

And there are other signs you should recognize, such as:

— when seated in a restaurant, you scan the menu before the waitress;

— when you find a bucket seat doesn't always fit the bucket;

— when you agree men are attracted to two types of women — those who wear well, and those who wear little;

— when you've learned that race horses, women, and fish are smarter than you are;

— when you've gotten enough experience to watch your step, only to find you aren't going anywhere;

But don't worry, for every time you're a year older, so is everyone else. It might surprise you to learn that Mickey Mouse is now forty-seven, Little Orphan Annie is fifty-one, Blondie forty-five, Dick Tracy forty-four, Li'l Abner forty, Superman thirty-seven, and even Charlie Brown is twenty-five.

Naturally your own birthday is something special, but close to nine million other people on this planet share it with you. So enjoy life by accepting aging as a normal process, rather than making a production of it. Growing old is something anybody can accomplish if he has the time.

Chapter 9

Preparing for retirement.

As retirement approaches, you can ease the wife's mind by telling her of all the expenses that will be eliminated when that time comes. No more income tax and Social Security deductions. No more lunches, charity contributions, and collections for every cause. Half as many hair cuts and fewer shoe shines. No beer with the boys once in a while. Fewer cleaning costs since you will need fewer fresh shirts, ties, and pressed suits. So add them up. (If there are other items, such as taking a girl friend out to lunch now and then, you don't have to mention them.)

With all those savings, you can readily see that you don't really

have to make definite financial plans for retirement. And what with Social Security, maybe a modest pension, and perhaps a little income from a few investments, these should be sufficient to allow you to putter around the garden, and mutter around the house. But it wouldn't hurt to consider a few Do's and Dont's for the years leading up to that period of life.

Whether you can take it with you isn't so much a problem as to whether you can hold on to it until you go. So do beware of the chap who reminds you that you can't take it with you. Given the chance, he'll take it with him!

Don't live life like some people play a slot machine — by trying to put in as little as possible and always hoping to hit the jackpot. If you must gamble, gamble on yourself. We are all manufacturers — making goods, making trouble, or making excuses. If you want to retire rich, start your own business manufacturing crutches for lame excuses. You know there's always a better way to produce anything — except children.

Don't worry too much about automation taking over your job before you retire. Remember that whenever a traffic jam gets really bad, they turn off the traffic lights and bring in a policeman. Be guided by the thought that life is like a game of bridge — only a dummy puts all his cards on the table.

Drive carefully! Remember, it's not only a car that can be recalled by its maker. And don't pattern your life like some people who wouldn't hesitate to drive up to the gates of heaven itself and honk.

Follow Mark Twain's advice: "Don't go around saying the world owes you a living; the world owes you nothing — it was here first." If the world did owe us a living, we wouldn't be shipped into it C.O.D.

Give some thought to the philosophy of the fellow who did odd jobs to supplement his income. "I never work on Sundays, except for the Lord," he said to a friend.

"What's the pay?" he was asked jokingly.

After a pause, he retorted, "Well, the pay isn't so hot, but you can't beat *that* retirement plan."

Do every job as if you were the boss. Drive as if all the other vehicles around you were police cars. Treat everybody as if he were you. And above all, don't stop trying — it's always the last key you try that opens the lock. We all admire the fellow who never gives up — almost as much as we like the chap who knows when to quit.

On the money side, never lend money to a friend — you may damage his memory. Never invest in anything that eats or needs repainting. Never buy anything with a handle on it — it means work. Remember, the quickest way to lose your shirt is to put too much on the cuff. A nice garden may be in your retirement plans, but keep in mind that gardening didn't keep Adam out of mischief.

As a retiree, you know you will have less income so, if you're a shrewd husband, try to convince your wife that a 30-day charge account can be used only in April, June, September, and November. And you don't have to be retired to know that a wife with a revolving charge account can really send her husband spinning. Before spending money for anything, always ask yourself, "If it takes two to make a bargain, why is it that only one gets it?" Man is the only animal that can be skinned more than once.

Chapter 10.

After retirement.

Beware of those brochures extolling the wonderful life for retirees in another area. You might retire to a place where you felt so good you'd want to work again — and you wouldn't want that to happen, would you? Remember, ours seems to be the only nation on earth that asks its teenagers what to do about world affairs, and then tells its golden-agers to go out and play.

Whether you move or not, the adjustment to retirement living will be gradual. Working and living have been synonymous too long for their separation to occur overnight. Instead, the transition will probably cover three distinct periods of one's retirement years.

First, there comes a period of frustration. A neighbor who retired

recently voiced this very well when he complained, "I wake up in the morning with nothing to do, and go to bed with it only half done." This sort of person hasn't learned to play yet, as retirees are supposed to do, and finds adjustment difficult because he has too much idle time on his hands. He needs a reason for getting out of the house and an opportunity to prove to himself that his time is still of some value. If he enjoys music, and really likes to meet people, he'll find that a temporary job as a bill collector is just what the doctor ordered. Almost everyone he visits will sing the blues — and ask him to call again.

During the second period, the retiree pushes the ugly thought of work farther away. This change of attitude is expressed by a fellow who keeps a list of house and yard chores posted on the ceiling of his home workshop. When asked why, he explains simply, "Because I hardly ever look there."

Lounging around the house all day in his easy chair, a fellow might hear his wife answer someone at the door with: "No, we're not a retired couple. We're a retired man and his wife." To offset such possiblities a man, for his own good, must keep a little spot where he can be himself without reserve. In solitude alone can he know true freedom.

And during the third period comes a note of finality, as expressed by Mr. McDale while discussing the mysteries of life with some friends. "I'm going deaf and blind," he sighed. "I don't know what the good Lord wants to leave me here for."

"Now, Mr. McDale," replied a friend, "the Lord's ways are not our ways and we can't understand them. But if He left you here, He's got work for you to do."

Mr. McDale sat for a minute in quiet meditation, then answered, "Well, I'm not a-gonna do it!"

If your wife doesn't treat you as you deserve — be thankful.

While a man is on the job, marriage is mostly an evening and weekend proposition and the wife feels she is ruler of the household. She is satisfied with a man *around* the house, but not with a man *in* the house to invade her domain on a twenty-four hour basis. So, after retirement, a man must adjust to his wife's routine where the home is concerned, rather than expecting her to be at his beck and call.

Researchers, interviewing wives, have reported that only one wife in five said she had no complaints about her husband. This ratio certainly won't improve after retirement if more wives find their husbands under foot most of the time. It is still generally true that the ideal husband is the one next door, especially if it is noticed he knows when to make himself scarce during the day.

Chapter 11

Retirement and your health.

After retirement, there is no real need to pamper yourself. A food statistician has reported that during an individual's lifetime, he eats 30,000 eggs, 6,000 loaves of bread, 9,000 pounds of potatoes, 8,000 pounds of beef, 12 sheep, 15 pigs, 5 calves, and 9,000 pounds of fish. Over a seventy year span you'll probably eat 1,400 times your body weight, so what earthly difference can a few pieces of pie make?

Forget those scientists who say we are what we eat. If that were true, nuts would be a more common diet than we had thought. But putting on weight is like inflation — it's easier to start than to stop. About the only time excess weight will make a man feel better is

when he sees it on a girl he nearly married. And many of us don't know what poor losers we are until we try dieting.

It should help you watch your intake if you keep in mind that the more body weight you carry around, the shorter time you'll be likely to have to carry it. Every pound of excess weight you carry makes it necessary for your heart to pump blood through more than three miles of blood vessels it wouldn't have to serve otherwise. Then, too, you're kept alive by only a third of the food you eat — the other two-thirds keeps the doctors alive.

As for drinking, one of life's puzzling oddities is that every centenarian has either used alcoholic beverages most of his life, or has let them completely alone. Whatever your taste, the following comparison of liquid costs, compiled by a municipality not so long ago, should be interesting:

Municipal water	20 cents per ton
Pop	$210 per ton
Beer	$405 per ton
Whisky, 100 proof	$6144 per ton

True, the costs are higher today, but the percentage of one to another should be about the same.

The trouble with taking a drink is that it makes a new man of you — and then the new man wants a drink. However, of all the remedies that absolutely won't cure a cold, whisky is by far the most popular. As one wife said to her husband, "Well, if you're not breaking up your cold germs, at least you're showing them a good time!" So take your choice — you still have years ahead of you.

If you have been living it up a little too much, don't be like the fellow who said to his doctor, "I didn't come in to be told I'm burning the candle at both ends. I came in for more wax." A person who burns the candle at both ends may not be as bright as he thinks. Accept your doctor's diagnosis, for it could be that your chief trouble is nothing more than milestones.

If your doctor says you have a go-go mind in a so-so body, believe him. You can even get a little comfort if, after a checkup, the doctor says, "You'll have to give up wine and women — but you can sing as much as you want to." Well, go ahead and sing! Just don't continue the elderly playboy roll and have people say, "He's reached the age where he chases girls only if it's down hill."

If you should go to the hospital for a little stitching, remember you are covered by Medicare. So, after the operation, don't be surprised if there is a little sign pasted next to the incision reading: "This is a Federal Project showing your tax dollars at work."

To keep in good health you should exercise, but only moderately. Without straining yourself, you can lift your eyebrows; jump to conclusions; stretch the truth; dig up some facts; box a compass; run around in circles; or run up some bills. And if you are clever, you may be able to throw your weight around without losing your balance. But two things are bad for the heart — running upstairs and running down people.

Even if you don't follow any of the suggestions above, you will get a certain amount of exercise. For, as an adult of average weight during a twenty-four stretch, you will: exercise 7 million brain cells; speak 4,800 words — each word requiring the use of 72 muscles; breathe 23,040 times; move 650 muscles; and inhale 438 cubic feet of air.

If you feel dog tired at night, it may be because you growled all day. On such occasions, when every bone in your body aches, just be thankful you have only 226 bones, and not all those of a herring. Smile at the world and echo the words of the old mountaineer: "I'm still kickin', but I ain't raisin' any dust." A few aches and pains aren't so bad as long as you have regular eliminations without the use of salts, oils, mineral waters, or enemas.

Chapter 12.

Enjoying retirement.

Of course you want to enjoy your retirement. Who doesn't? So accept the fact that fun can be compared to life insurance — the older you get, the more it costs. But since a person is never too old to yearn, choose your pleasure wisely. A pint of enjoyment can equal a peck of trouble; and there's still time to pay a fat figure for getting involved with a slim one.

You'll find that everybody and his brother urge retired persons to take up a hobby, which is something you go goofy over to keep from going nuts about things in general. Virtually everything possible is recommended as a hobby except the most enjoyable of all — namely, loafing. As one person put it, "There's nothing disgraceful about planned loafing — if you can afford it."

If, unfortunately, you have become somewhat deaf, invest in

one of those hearing aids concealed in your glasses, but don't let others know about it. One fellow who did this returned to the store to express his delight, saying, "Am I having fun! In the past week I've changed my will twice."

And don't put off having your eyes tested. They control 80 per cent of our actions, are responsible for 82 per cent of our learning, yet seeing consumes only about 25 per cent of the energy our bodies create. So if you need bifocals, or even trifocals, by all means get them, for they are not a sign of age. They are simply one way of telling the world you're still young enough not to want to miss anything going on around you.

In retirement, as when you had a steady job, it is not difficult to meet expenses — they're everywhere. But if you meet them successfully to the end, you will have the final pleasure of knowing there will be no message on your tombstone such as the one that read: "Owen Moore Has Gone Away, Owin' More Than He Could Pay." The stone was erected by his creditors.

With more leisure (if you can keep others from using it up on you), you should get more enjoyment and inspiration from reading your Bible. Don't mind if you overhear someone remark that he thinks you are cramming for your finals. He would be wrong indeed if you were only looking for loopholes. And you'll find more pleasure comes from confiding in God, for you know He doesn't gossip.

In the same vein, how about going to church a little more often? By the time a person has reached seventy, some scientists claim he has spent approximately twenty-four years sleeping, eleven years working, eight years at recreation, six years eating, five and one-half years washing and dressing, three years talking, and only six months in church.

Although many a man's idea of a good sermon is one that goes over his head and hits a neighbor, it can help people in many ways. Some rise from such a sermon greatly strengthened; others wake up from it refreshed. Regardless of your personal reaction, you could help bring up the average for reasons like that of the fellow who said, "Each time I pass a church, I stop to pay a visit, so that when I am carried in, the Lord won't ask, 'Who is it?' "

One of the delights known to age — and beyond the grasp of youth — is that of "not going" somewhere. But if you do go, one trip will probably be to the old class reunion, if only for the purpose of getting together to see who is falling apart. And what do you notice most? One fellow said it was, "The same old faces, but more new teeth."

Sir Winston Churchill once said, "We are happier in many ways when we are old than when we were young. The young sow wild oats. The old grow sage." You yourself can admire the wisdom of those who come to you for advice because then you can brag about your own youth with less likelihood of being contradicted.

As the years pass, you will enjoy them more if you have some particular reason to which you can attribute your longevity. One old-timer said that he attributed his: . . . "to automobiles — I never git in the way of them."

And a hearty fellow nearing ninety once said: "I reckon it's because many a night I went to bed and slept, when I should have sat up and worried."

One wealthy lady, when asked why she thought God had permitted her to reach the age of ninety, replied without hesitation: "To test the patience of my relatives."

Most of us seem to live far beyond our allotted time, judging by the "lifetime guarantees" we outlast. But if you are enjoying life and want to continue longer than most, there are two aids at your disposal:

(1) Keep the corners of your mouth turned upward. For although it is strange when you think of it, of all the countless folk who have lived on this planet not one is known in history or legend as having died of laughter. Then, too, if you keep smiling, it makes everybody wonder what you've been up to.

(2) Break a mirror. Regardless of what else lies ahead, it is supposed to mean that at least you'll last another seven years.

There is always the possibility that somewhere along the line you'll feel as if you're in your second childhood. You'll get the urge to dye your hair, grow a beard, or wear a toupee to help bring back that younger look. Indeed, not since the days of Indian scalp gathering have so many people been going around with hair that isn't their own, so the desire for a toupee is understandable.

This urge to be different isn't new to man, for history verifies that men were the first to curl their hair, apply cosmetics, don silk stockings, and wear high heels. So, if the urge is strong enough, why try to fight history?

Everybody needs memories, for they keep the wolf of insignificance away from the door. The older you become, the more you will treasure memories of years gone by. And it's wonderful that everyone has 20/20 hindsight.

Some people find that living in the past has one thing in its favor — it's cheaper. Others like the old days because that's when they were younger. You'll smile to yourself if you can remember way back when it was the fashion to take one bath weekly — and religion daily. Or, if you can recall such comments as, "Virtues are learned at mother's knee, vices at some other joint." Yes, how times have changed!

Looking back, one retired fellow recalled, "The richest I have ever been was when I was a boy and found a five dollar bill. It's the only time in my life I ever had enough money to buy more than I wanted. I guess you can't get any richer than that."

Another old-timer reminisced: "I was born on Main Street. Lived there before the town macadamized it, before Henry Ford motorized it, before the unions organized it, before the chain stores standardized it, and before the federal government subsidized it."

Still another oldster, who seemed very contented with life, was heard to comment: "Yes, sir, I'll be ninety tomorrow, and I haven't an enemy in the world." "A beautiful thought," replied his visitor. "Yes sir," the oldster continued, "I've outlived them all."

And there was the elderly lady watching a number of antique automobiles displayed in a parade. After they had all passed by, she was heard to exclaim, "Oh, they're so lovely. I've had a good time in every one of them."

After reading the will of a career girl who had passed on at age eighty-seven, it was learned that memories had influenced her to include the clause: "I don't want anyone to put 'Miss' on my tombstone — I haven't missed as much as some people might think."

A most beautiful thought was expressed by a lady who had grown old ever so sweetly when she was asked, "How does it feel to be eighty-five years old?" Her face lighted up as she replied, "Oh, it's just like Saturday afternoon on the farm when all the work is done, and you're ready for Sunday."

Memories provide opportunities to relive moments and associations with others we have enjoyed, and it is satisfying to recall those for which we are thankful. For example, any man can give thanks if in his lifetime he has found one wife, one friend, and one cigarette lighter he could depend upon.

Chapter 13.

Conclusions.

Until we reach senior citizenship status, we are slaves — slaves to rules, regulations, and regimentation. As babies, we eat when the time comes to feed us. When we grow older, we keep the hours and follow the rules laid out for us. When we get a job, we are subject to rules and regulations.

All through life for sixty-five years, or whenever retirement comes, we are subject to the will of other people. Then comes the best time, as we more fully comprehend the beauty of Robert Browning's words: "Grow old along with me! The best is yet to be. The last of life for which the first was made."

Yet the way the word "retire" is bandied about today, you could apply it to almost any change you've ever made. You could say

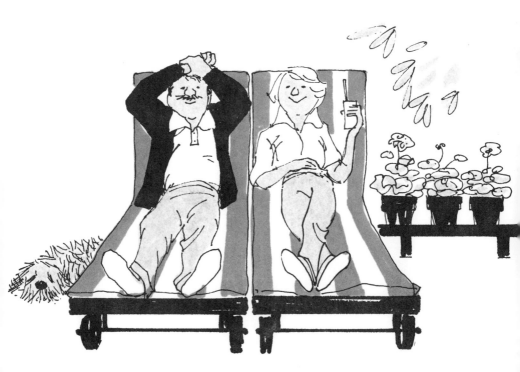

that you retire from the eighth grade to enter high school; you retire from high school to enter college or take a job; you retire from bachelorhood to get married; you retire from Illinois to move to Indiana; you retire from an hourly pay job to become a supervisor. And you retire every night to go to bed. So what's new about retiring?

A company doesn't retire you as an individual, but as an employee. It also retires bonds, stock, notes, and machinery. When you and your job part ways, you aren't retiring from the human race — you're merely making another change, move, or transfer. You're retiring from a straitjacket life style to become, for the first time, your own boss of your own time. The question you have to answer is: What are you going to do with it?

Whether you have already made a name for yourself or not, here are some words of comfort from researchers who have looked into the histories of some forty famous men, each one the most outstanding statesman, painter, warrior, poet, or writer of his time. Of this group's greatest achievements, 35 per cent came when the men were between sixty and seventy; 23 per cent when they were between seventy and eighty; and eight per cent when they were more than eighty. In other words, sixty-six per cent of the world's greatest work has been done by men past sixty. Feel better?

Cato, the Roman statesman, started to study Greek when he was around eighty. Someone asked why he was beginning so large a task at such an advanced age. Cato replied drily that it was the youngest age he had left.

And at age seventy-five, his international reputation as a virtuoso long since established, Pablo Casals was asked why he continued to practice the cello four hours each day. "Because," he answered, "I think I am making some progress."

So *you* don't want to study Greek or play the cello. Do you just plan to sit on your front porch and listen to your arteries harden? Of course not. Actually, hardening of the *attitudes* starts long before hardening of the arteries, and you haven't let that happen to you, have you? There are so many new friendships to be made, so many things to do that you've never had time for before. What you need to do is get involved! Circulate! Give people a chance to say, "I'm glad to know you!" No one has less to live for than one who lives only for himself.

Think of it this way: your next role will be that of an ancestor. Now that *is* worth thinking about, for when you reach this stage, whatever was yours will belong to another, whatever you were will belong to you. Of course, a miser makes a good ancestor, but you've never had the inclination to be one. If you had, you probably would have worried a lot trying to decide whether to take long steps and save shoe leather, or short steps so as not to strain any of the stitches in your pants. And who wants to live with such weighty problems to be solved every day?

So, what else could you be pleasantly remembered for? Of several possibilities, there is one in particular that all your descendants should prize very highly — and that is a family history. To be ignorant of the past is to remain a child, so why not appoint yourself Family Historian and give it to them?

Whatever your lineage, your family has played its part in the growth of our wonderful nation. You can give your descendants a stronger feeling of belonging by bringing them closer to their ancestors who have, each in his own way, helped make it so. To become a good ancestor, how better could you spend part of what you have the mostest of — your time?